CAREER AS A
KINDERGARTEN TEACHER

EARLY CHILDHOOD EDUCATION

KINDERGARTEN TEACHERS HAVE THE AWESOME JOB of instructing young children, between the ages of five and six, during their first year of school. This is the most important year in a student's life as they are building the foundation needed for future education. It is also the most challenging level to teach. Welcome to the world of finger paints, storybooks, play-acting, and circle time. Welcome to the Big K!

Kindergarten teachers prepare students for higher grades by providing instruction in basic subjects. The children may start with little or no knowledge at all of letters and numbers. By the time they move up to first grade, they will be able to read, write, and perform simple calculations among other things. This intellectual growth occurs through play and hands-on learning. A typical classroom may look like an indoor playground, but each activity is carefully structured to convey a lesson.

Academics aside, there is much more to teaching kindergarten than singing songs and reciting the ABCs. Kindergarten teachers are also responsible for teaching social skills and personal hygiene. At this age, children are unaware of the many rules surrounding social interaction within a group dynamic. They must learn how to take turns, raise their hands before speaking, line up, and put things away. They may also need help with tying shoes, buttoning coats, or blowing their nose. It is safe to say that kindergarten teachers are the most important educators a child will ever have.

It takes special knowledge and skills to impart lifelong learning skills to young children. Kindergarten teachers must have at least a bachelor's degree. The most common major is early childhood education, though there are other possibilities. A teacher preparation program, which is essentially an internship with specialized training, is also required. This is usually completed during undergraduate study. After graduation, public school teachers must pass an exam and obtain a state-issued certification or license before working in a classroom. Many private schools do not require a license.

New kindergarten teachers may find it challenging to land their first job. Job openings normally occur once a year and are usually filled in spring for the following fall session. It takes careful planning and patience, but kindergarten teachers with the right combination of training, references, and enthusiasm will find that they are needed in both public and private schools.

The pay is lower compared to other professions with comparable educational requirements. Most salaries range from $50,000 to $70,000 a year. It looks a little better when considering teachers are off duty for two months in the summer, three weeks in the winter, and one or two weeks in the spring. The benefits are also good, with exceptional health coverage and retirement plans. Clearly, kindergarten teachers do not enter this career for the money. They do it because they love children and are passionate about education and helping their young charges get off to the best possible start in their academic lives.

WHAT YOU CAN DO NOW

KINDERGARTEN TEACHERS MUST EARN a bachelor's degree to be eligible for a license. In high school, classes that prepare you for college should be a priority. Keep in mind that your high school graduation requirements may differ from college admission requirements. Check with the admissions office of the colleges you are considering for specific course requirements. Ask your school counselor to help you create a good high school plan.

Consider taking some advanced courses in high school, if available. You may receive college credit for Advanced Placement (AP) and International Baccalaureate (IB) courses, if you do well in them.   At the very least, they will add weight to your college application.

Look for electives that would be helpful in preparing you for this profession. These might include classes in child development, psychology, safety and first aid, parenting, and art.

Visit a kindergarten classroom. Seeing one in action is the best way to determine if you are truly suited for this career. Try to arrange a job shadow. The opportunity to observe, talk to, and learn from an experienced kindergarten teacher is invaluable. Check with your counselor to see if there are any other work-based learning opportunities available in your school.

Get some experience working with young children. Babysitting jobs are easy to come by. Up your game and prepare some age-appropriate activities that are fun yet educational. Look into volunteering as a teacher's assistant at a local school or childcare facility.

You might also be able to land a part-time or summer job at a private preschool or kindergarten. Teachers at these schools who work during the regular school year like to take a significant amount of time off during the summer. Since most of these schools do offer summer programs, they are often left scrambling to fill positions with temporary help.

HISTORY OF THE PROFESSION

THE WORLD'S FIRST KINDERGARTEN WAS established in 1837 in Bad Blankenburg, a village in East Germany. The founder, Friedrich Froebel, was a pedagogue and student of Johann Pestalozzi, the Swiss educational reformer. Pestalozzi's influence cannot be overstated. He laid the foundation for modern education, based on his belief that children have unique needs and capabilities. Following up on this philosophy, Froebel created the concept of kindergarten (meaning "garden of children"), an educational institute where children would be nurtured and nourished "like plants in a garden."

Froebel's institute began as a social experiment for children entering school for the first time. The foundation of the concept was learning through play and activity, and Froebel had strong ideas about how that play should be presented. The kindergarten day would start with songs and continue on with a series of toys he designed for children who were too young for traditional schoolwork. He also believed that early education was an extension of mothering, and that children so young (age three to six) should, therefore, be taught only by women. Froebel trained many women to open kindergartens throughout Europe and elsewhere in the world.

Kindergarten Comes to America

The first kindergarten in the US was founded in Wisconsin by Margarethe Meyer-Schurz in 1856. Like other kindergartens opened by Froebel's students, classes were conducted in German. That same year, American teacher Elizabeth Peabody read an article about Froebel's methods in a magazine. She was intrigued by his educational philosophy, which aligned with her own. In her own work with young children, she rejected the common method of rote memorization and drills. Instead, she created games intertwined with physical activity to teach math, spelling, and grammar.

In 1860, Peabody and her sister, Mary Mann, opened the first English-language private kindergarten in the US. A few years later, Mann took over while Peabody went to Europe to train with Froebel and others. When she returned, Peabody became a spokesperson for the kindergarten movement, advocating for women to launch schools that would further the education philosophy that was considered by most educators at the time to be a revolutionary concept. Her first student was Susan Blow.

The First Public Kindergarten

The same Susan Blow, together with St. Louis school superintendent William Harris, opened the first public kindergarten in 1873. Their kindergarten was child--centric, following Froebel's rigid guidelines precisely. The Industrial Revolution was in full swing during the late 1800s, and many mothers joined the workforce. For the first time, mothers needed to find help to care for their young children. There was a growing number of teachers, like Peabody and Blow, ready to step in and meet the demand with supervision that went well beyond basic childrearing. By 1880, there were more than 400 kindergartens in 30 states, and schools for training kindergarten teachers were in every major American city. Free (publicly funded) kindergartens were especially popular, as they were considered neighborhood community centers.

By the early 1900s, the kindergarten movement had become very progressive. Froebel's strict rules evolved into new ideas and practices based on scientific principles. Unfortunately, the concern for the social development of children, an important feature of the first kindergartens, was lost as classrooms grew. To manage so many children, teachers had to teach double sessions and forego the close interactions with parents which they once had.

Kindergarten in the 20th Century

Every major city in the US had public kindergartens by 1920. The curriculum changed significantly in that decade. New subject areas were introduced, and learning objectives moved away from helping children adjust to the social environment of school. Research in early childhood education was on the rise, and new child study centers were opened at numerous universities. Studies focused on teachers' activities, looking for ways to increase efficiency. The result was a move toward standardization in the kindergarten curriculum.

For a time, public kindergarten and first grade programs were unified, serving a broad age range of three to seven. This changed as the new standards were integrated. The first grade curriculum was completely overhauled, and the kindergarten curriculum was made age appropriate for four to five year olds.

The 1950s saw a rising concern about preparing children for the workforce of the future. There was a demand for more academics in the kindergarten curriculum that would ensure students' future academic success. But by the 1960s, there was a backlash among many parents who wanted to return to the more natural learning methods that were much like those Froebel first established. The methods of Maria Montessori and Jean Piaget considered tactile and physical activity essential for the young learner. Still, there was tremendous pressure among education organizations to focus on rigorous academics in kindergartens.

Research was conducted to confirm that kindergarten academics correlated to academic success in later years. The number of subjects grew and soon everything from science to social studies was integrated throughout the day with various activities.

In 1983, the US Department of Education released the report, *A Nation at Risk,* which warned that Americans were failing to compete with the intellectual capacity of the Japanese. The report emphasized that education needed to be taken more seriously. As a result, there was a surge of public support for compulsory, tax supported kindergarten in all public schools. By the 1990s, enrollment of all five year olds had risen almost 100 percent, and kindergarten had become mandatory in 12 states and Washington DC.

A prevalent outcome of *A Nation at Risk* was the transformation of the kindergarten curriculum into a watered down version of first grade. With the expectation of increased academics, school readiness became an issue. In 1994, The Education America Act stated that all children would start first grade ready to learn. In response, many states raised the age of entrance into kindergarten, allowing for time in Pre-K for young children to prepare for the "real school" environment. In other states, parents would often hold back their children for a year in hopes that their children, being the oldest in class, would outperform their classmates academically.

Today's kindergarten curriculum is a full-day cognitive based program that seeks to have students reading and writing as they enter the first grade. Technology is present and integrated into the curriculum. Kindergarten is no longer seen as a place to get ready for school, but rather a place to learn and develop the social and academic foundation on which to build the academic future.

WHERE YOU WILL WORK

THERE ARE MORE THAN 160,000 kindergarten teachers in the US. They can be found working in one of three places: public schools, private schools, or charter schools. The vast majority work in public schools.

Public schools are free of charge, supported by state and federal funds. They are governed at three levels – by the US Department of Education, the state's board of education, and the local school district. Kindergarten teachers are employed by the local school district. The district also sets the guidelines for what occurs in the classroom, including the curriculum, textbooks, activities, etc. Teachers who work in public schools experience the most diversity with students coming from every ethnic and socioeconomic background.

Private schools are quickly rising in popularity. Currently, about one out of four kindergarten students attends a private school. Tuition is required since private schools do not receive public funding. Private schools are generally free to create their own curriculum since they are administered by private organizations, not the government. Most private schools have the same requirements for teachers, but there are some that do not require licensure.

In recent years, many charter schools have begun to offer kindergarten. Charter schools are independent public schools that do not require tuition, and have the freedom to design classrooms that meet students' needs. Classrooms are typically very small compared to a traditional public school, and the teaching standards are high. Generally, only teachers with a high level of experience, a master's degree, and proven expertise are hired by charter schools.

Work Environment

The kindergarten environment is usually bright, colorful, and mentally stimulating. One of the fun parts of the job is designing the classroom, which teachers are generally allowed to do as they see fit. Looking around the typical classroom, you will see pint-size tables and chairs, a large area rug for storytime and singalongs, shelves of books, easels for painting, musical instruments, cubbies for personal belongings, an assortment of (educational) games and puzzles, pictures of the students and their families, assorted posters on the walls, and a classroom pet. Depending on the school's budget, there may also be a computer center, theater setup with assorted costumes, kitchens, and separate napping areas with beds instead of roll-up mats.

Work Schedule

Kindergarten classes vary in length. They can be full time, part time, or something in between. They all start at about the same time, which is usually around 8:30 am. The exception is when there are two part-time classes, one morning and one afternoon. Part-time classes usually last for three hours, while full-time classes end between 2:30 and 3:00pm.

Kindergarten teachers also spend considerable time outside the classroom, meeting with parents or other teachers, and preparing lessons. Most public kindergarten teachers follow the traditional 10-month school year, with a two-month break during the summer. Breaks during the school year include several weeks during midwinter and one week in the spring. Private kindergarten teachers may follow the same schedule, but more often they work for about nine weeks, then take a break of one to three weeks before continuing. Private schools often offer the option for teachers to work during the summer if they choose.

THE WORK YOU WILL DO

KINDERGARTEN TEACHERS HAVE AN awesome responsibility. Since kindergarten is the first official year of school, it is their job to shape the first educational experience of young children and help establish the foundation for lifelong learning. Kindergarten students are usually only five or six years old, so they are naturally apprehensive and anxious at first. Unless they have been to a formal preschool, they often have no understanding of the basic rules and procedures of a classroom. It is up to the teacher to create a warm and welcoming environment.

Kindergarten teachers have multiple roles – teacher, role model, and substitute parent. The classroom instruction covers a variety of fundamental subjects, like basic numbers and letters, social studies, and natural science. Creative educational activities and tools are used, like games, music, art, stories, songs, theater, and computers. In addition to providing academic instruction, kindergarten teachers help develop and support students' physical and social skills. For example, they introduce students to classroom norms, such as raising hands, forming lines, taking turns, asking for permission to go to the restroom, speaking in an appropriate volume, participating in group activities, and other classroom behavior. Teachers also act as coaches and cheerleaders, offering encouragement to those lacking confidence.

The core task for any kindergarten teacher is lesson planning for each day and for the collective school year. The school district and/or school administration will dictate curriculum guidelines meant to meet learning goals. The kindergarten teacher works off of those guidelines, adapting and implementing the curriculum through play and hands-on learning.

Preparing a lesson plan could include any number of tasks, like selecting stories or songs, preparing art projects, pinning maps on the wall, creating educational games, decorating the classroom, gathering costumes, or distributing paper and pencils on every table. Since every lesson will be very new for the young learners, the challenge is to come up with fun and engaging activities that can be vehicles for learning. One of the most effective methods is integrating performing and visual arts into the curriculum.

Because kindergarten is all about building a foundation for future learning, instructions begin with the most simple concepts, and step by step, move on to more advanced ideas. For example, instruction may start with recognizing different shapes and colors, then on to letters of the alphabet and numbers one through ten. By the end of the school year, students will have built the skills to read and write simple sentences, and do simple addition and subtraction. Along the way they will learn to tell time, understand where they live, and acknowledge different peoples and customs. Every step will stimulate their critical thinking ability, making them capable of learning more advanced concepts.

Giving lessons can be tiring, especially since kindergarten teachers cannot just tell students to read a chapter in a textbook. Instructions are usually given while standing, or sometimes sitting on a rug during circle time, while singing a song or reading a story. There is lunchtime, recess, and sometimes naps, but these breaks are mostly for the children. Teachers have to supervise or use the time to plan lessons or call parents.

Other Core Tasks

In addition to classroom instruction, other key responsibilities include student assessment, participating in meetings and classroom management.

Evaluating academic and emotional development is important for ensuring that each individual student is making adequate progress. Kindergarten teachers continually test students' strengths and weaknesses. Based on their assessments, they will set individualized goals and modify lessons to overcome any identified learning challenges. Ideally, kindergarten teachers can instruct their students one-on-one or in very small groups, adapting their methods to meet students' varying needs and interests. That is not always possible though, especially when a class is overcrowded. They must observe and assess the performance of the class as a whole, and make adjustments to the lesson plans as needed. They also watch for any potential health, emotional, behavioral or social development issues.

The most effective kindergarten teachers are very good at keeping in touch with parents, and working together to support the development of students. Some teachers like to send emails to parents every few days, or when the child has done something great – or not so great. Others send out weekly newsletters that summarize what has happened in the classroom during the week. Some will make a point of meeting and chatting with parents when they come to pick up their child, or even visit the home on occasion.

Regardless of what an individual teacher does to build relationships with parents, periodic parent-teacher conferences are required. They typically take place three or four times a year. These meetings are meant to update parents on their child's progress and to inform them of any concerns. If there are any problem areas, the teacher and parents can work together to come up with a plan of action that will help the child reach full potential.

Kindergarten teachers also attend regular staff meetings to discuss school-related news and activities. These meetings generally take place during the school day, giving the students a day off.

Learning to manage a classroom full of young children is perhaps the hardest lesson for a kindergarten teacher. It is extremely important to be able to maintain a safe, well-organized classroom that supports an optimal learning environment for every student. There are usually school guidelines for classroom management. For kindergarten teachers, they usually specify monitoring interactions in the classroom to ensure there is sharing, mutual respect, and positivity among the students.

Non-Teaching Tasks

Because kindergarten students are very young and often experiencing school for the first time, the job of a kindergarten teacher is different from that of other teachers. Teaching students how to read, write, and do basic math is sometimes the easiest part of the job. The harder part is teaching them how to behave in the classroom environment. Being able to maintain order in the classroom is dependent on children learning and following the general rules of acceptable behavior. First-time students need to learn how to play nicely with others within a group as well as work quietly on their own.

In addition, these very young children often need help with basic daily activities. For example, kindergarten teachers often help button coats, tie shoes, dry tears, and blow noses. One of their yearly goals is to teach the children to accomplish these tasks on their own.

TALES OF TEACHERS

I Teach Kindergarten in a Public School

"I love teaching kindergarten. I have taught other grades as well, but kindergarten is my favorite. When people learn what I do, they often remark that it must be fun. It is fun, but it is also hard. For starters, the current standards for kindergarteners to move on to the first grade are way beyond what most people realize. They don't just learn to count their fingers and sing the ABC song. They need to fluently add and subtract within 10, read simple books, and write full sentences. If a student is struggling, I can't go back to the basics like I did with older kids. Kindergarten is the basics, and that is the hardest of all to teach.

In my classroom, you will see games, costumes, a kitchen, easels, Legos, and other toys. It looks like we play all day. We do have fun, but the play is very well planned and focused. With each activity, children are learning science, geography, math, phonemic awareness, and patterning. They are also building fine motor skills and learning all kinds of life skills. One can't underestimate the importance of play at this age.

The real challenge in teaching kindergarten isn't academics. Imagine getting 25 five-year-olds to follow you in a line somewhere. It takes a lot of train songs and practice to pull that off. There are so many other things kindergarteners don't know how to do, too. I teach them how to converse with classmates, take turns, put things away, and manage their emotions. Those things aren't easy to teach. Add lesson planning, evaluations, conferences, and paperwork, and my work is never really done.

In the end, my job is to help these young children grow and learn how to navigate the world of school. It is a challenge I gladly accept. I can't really imagine doing anything else!"

I Am a Traveling Teacher

"My passion has always been teaching, but I also have an itchy foot. After working as a teaching assistant in an elementary school for two years, I started to wonder if there was a way I could combine teaching and travel. Talking to a friend who had taught English in Japan for a year, I was surprised to learn that many countries are desperate for English teachers. With the help of an agency, I immediately landed my first contract. I booked my flight and I was off to China for 10 months. I have since taught in Poland, Cambodia, Thailand, and the Czech Republic.

Teaching English in kindergarten is a different experience. I don't stay with one class all day. Instead, I have more than 100 students every day, spread between six classes of two to six year olds. The most difficult part is remembering all their names.

Little kids are the same everywhere – cute, adorable, and great fun. They all want to play, jump, dance, and laugh. I use that to my advantage, teaching them through games and exercises. Luckily, I am allowed to bring my own ideas to make classes more effective. By the end of the year, it is amazing how well they speak English, even though the youngest aren't yet completely fluent in their own language.

Teaching abroad offers more adventure and less stress. There is little competition for jobs, you are in charge of your class, and everyone from coworkers to parents are very helpful and supportive. The pay is excellent and I usually get accommodations and food, too."

I Teach in a Charter School

"After teaching in a public kindergarten for 10 years, I learned of a new charter school that was opening in a nearby city. I was intrigued because it was to be located in a disadvantaged community. The idea of providing an 'ideal' learning environment to underprivileged children stuck in my head. When I got the news that I had been accepted for a kindergarten position, I was both excited and nervous.

Most of my students are children of recent immigrants from several different countries. One of the advantages of working in a charter school versus a traditional school is having the freedom to weave diverse cultural features into my everyday curriculum. It helps me to make strong connections with my young students and create a safe environment for them to thrive.

There are many reasons why charter schools can sometimes accomplish what public schools cannot, like smaller classes, more resources, and increased accountability. But it's the freedom that really makes a difference. As teachers, we have the freedom to set our own academic goals and push standards higher than those of the district. With smaller classes and full-time aides, I can ensure that all of my children's needs are met so they can achieve their highest potential for academic success.

Because kindergarten will likely determine whether these children will succeed or fail in their school careers and perhaps even in life, I feel an urgent sense of responsibility to be the best teacher I can be. Each school year brings new challenges, quandaries, and stress. But at the end of the year, I am rewarded when I say good-bye to students who can now speak, write, and read so well."

PERSONAL QUALIFICATIONS

KINDERGARTEN IS THE FIRST FORMAL YEAR of education, which makes it a pivotal time in a child's academic life. So what does it take to get kids off to a good start? To be effective in the classroom, teachers need to be skilled in curriculum development, classroom management, lesson planning, and explaining new concepts to young learners. These are all practical skills that every teacher learns in college. What sets the most effective teachers apart are certain other characteristics that may be innate or developed over time.

Passion

Teaching is not always easy. Kindergarten teachers who are passionate about nurturing the minds of young children have the motivation to get them through the challenging times. It is not enough to like children. You need to love them and have a strong desire to make a difference in their lives.

Patience

Children in kindergarten are learning more than the alphabet. They are being introduced to rules and social norms in a group setting, often for the first time. They may not know how to deal with so many other children in the same space. They can be unpredictable, sweet and cute one minute and suddenly disruptive the next. At that age, they are also easily distracted and prone to being cranky and whiny when they are tired, hungry, or stressed. It takes exceptional patience to handle any behavior issues that may come up without getting stressed yourself.

Creativity

Kindergarten students need a warm and welcoming environment that also gets their attention. Most teachers are able to provide that with imaginative and inventive ideas that stimulate and engage young children. Where there are limited resources, extra creativity is needed to find ways around a tight budget. Creativity is also needed for planning lessons. Creative lessons and activities can greatly reduce behavior problems.

High Energy

Keeping up with five-year-olds can be a challenge. Kids this age come to school full of energy and excitement. The best kindergarten teachers can match their students' energy and channel it into enthusiasm for learning. Young children are kinesthetic learners, gathering and retaining information as they move around and jump in and out of their seats. The teachers are up and moving with them, demonstrating that school is fun. Prepare to be exhausted at the end of the day!

Communications Skills

Excellent communications skills, both spoken and written are essential. To keep students engaged, kindergarten teachers must be animated and able to convey new ideas and information in clear terms they can understand. Students come from all different cultures and backgrounds, something to remember when addressing an individual or the whole class. Teachers also need to be good listeners, alert for any signs of distress or confusion that could interfere with learning. Teachers must also keep the lines of communication open with parents.

Writing skills will come in handy every day while writing notes to parents, progress reports, and more.

ATTRACTIVE FEATURES

KINDERGARTEN TEACHERS CHOOSE THIS CAREER for one primary reason: they love children. Indeed, children are the best part of the job. Five-year-old children are excited by anything and everything new. They are very inquisitive and surprisingly good problem solvers. They are happy to share their thoughts on most any topic, and the things they come up with will either amaze you or make you laugh.

Compared to any other grade, there is more growth in kindergarten in a single school year. Kindergarten students are like sponges, soaking up everything you teach them. They come in not knowing how to write their name or count without fingers. They leave at the end of the year, able to read, write sentences, and count to 100. All along the way, it is deeply rewarding to see their eyes light up each time they "get it" or do something, such as read a sentence, for the very first time.

Kindergarten teachers in public schools usually receive a generous package of fringe benefits. Specific benefits can vary depending on the specific school and region, but comprehensive medical coverage and retirement plans are the norm. In some areas of the country, kindergarten teachers are offered extras, like help with home mortgages. These and other enticements are usually used to attract candidates where severe teacher shortages exist.

Kindergarten teachers do not have to work evenings, weekends, or holidays. Teaching is the one profession where individuals get lengthy breaks – two or three months in the summer, three weeks in the winter, a week in the spring, as well as personal days throughout the year. Although teachers spend a considerable amount of personal time preparing lessons, their schedules are convenient for raising a family. They usually have the same days off as their children and can easily plan holiday and summer vacations together.

Kindergarten teachers are not limited to teaching five--year-olds. As licensed teachers, they are qualified to teach any grade level in elementary school.

UNATTRACTIVE ASPECTS

AS FUN AS YOUNG KIDS ARE, TEACHING kindergarten is not always easy. In fact, handling a class full of energetic young children – especially when there is overcrowding – can be exhausting. You will be on your feet most of the day because kids this age cannot yet read textbooks. Instead, instruction is mostly oral. While the kids are getting a break during recess, you are still on your feet supervising. The workday is not over when the final bell rings either. There are lessons plans to make, parent emails to answer, reports to complete, and seminars to attend.

Pay for teachers is notoriously low. In fact, teacher salaries in many areas are well below the national average for all workers. School districts have to work with the money that is appropriated by legislatures and too often, education is the first item on the chopping block when there is an economic squeeze. When school districts are strapped for cash, there are additional disincentives to teaching – a lack of supplies, reduced benefits, and increased class sizes created by layoffs.

There is little job security or stability in the teaching field. Once a school year starts, you know what you are doing until June, but you never know for sure what will happen after that. There is no tenure for kindergarten teachers. You might have a job next year or you might need to dust off your résumé and start job hunting again.

There is more to the job of working with kindergarten students than teaching them to read and write. Five-year-olds are not old enough to be fully self-sufficient. They still need help with basic activities, like putting on coats, finding their lunches, tying shoes, getting to the bathroom, and blowing their noses. Many have not attended preschool or any other organized group activity. They need to be taught how to behave in a structured environment.

EDUCATION AND TRAINING

THE PATH TOWARD BECOMING A kindergarten teacher in the United States is fairly straightforward. Since kindergarten is the first year of primary education, teacher training is the same as for all other elementary school teachers. The specific requirements vary somewhat among different states, but the four basic steps are as follows:

- Earn a bachelor's degree

- Complete a teacher preparation program

- Pass a state exam

- Obtain a license

Note that these are the steps for teachers in the public school system. Private schools usually (but not always) require a bachelor's degree as well, but a state teaching license is not always required.

Bachelor's Degree

Kindergarten teachers ordinarily major in elementary education, early childhood education, child development, or a closely related subject. The selection of a major may be dependent on specific state licensing requirements, but any program that focuses on the needs and development of young learners is usually acceptable.

Elementary or early childhood education degree programs typically cover the "3 R's" – basic math, reading, and writing, plus children's art and literature. Much of the focus is on teaching techniques and methodologies. There will be generalized instruction in how to instruct young students in these subjects, as well as more specific teaching courses, like technology integration in the classroom, teaching students with special needs, and teaching in a multicultural classroom.

Master's Degree

It is not uncommon for professionals in other fields to switch careers and go into teaching. Those with a bachelor's degree in a subject other than education can fulfill licensing requirements by completing a master's degree in education that focuses on teaching young learners. There are many such programs that are specifically designed for transitioning from a non-teaching field to teaching young students.

A master's degree is also a good option for experienced teachers who wish to conduct educational research, specialize in a particular type of teaching (such as special education), or simply to enhance their career potential.

Teacher Preparation Program

Most states require prospective teachers to complete an accredited teacher preparation program. This is a non-degree certification program that includes an internship and specialized courses. Programs are usually completed during undergraduate study, but there are also some programs designed specifically for students who are returning to school after graduation. Applicants usually need a minimum 2.5 grade point average and in some cases need to complete an introductory course.

The coursework in teacher preparation programs is focused on the grade level and subjects that aspiring teachers are interested in. Typical classes for kindergarten teachers would cover childhood development, educational psychology, early childhood methods, language and literacy, and student assessment.

The internship part of the program is a one or two semester student teaching practicum. During this time, student teachers are in an actual classroom being mentored by an experienced kindergarten teacher. In-classroom experience is invaluable for honing skills, such as managing a classroom, writing effective lesson plans, instructing and evaluating students, and communicating with parents. To qualify for licensure, student teachers must be evaluated on their performance.

Teaching Exam

The final requirement before applying for a state license to teach is passing the necessary competency exams given to every elementary school teacher. Every state develops or adopts its own exam, but they are generally the same in subject matter. Many states use the Pre-Professional Skills Test (PPST) or Praxis tests, which are considered the national standard for assessing qualifications.

Licensing

All states require kindergarten teachers to be licensed before teaching in a public school. Each state has its own specific licensing requirements, which can be obtained by contacting any particular state's Board of Education. Generally, once a prospective kindergarten teacher has earned an acceptable bachelor's degree, completed the teacher preparation program, and passed the required state exams, they are ready to apply for a license to teach in their state. In addition to the educational requirements, they must also submit fingerprints and pass a criminal background check.

Voluntary Certification Options

Kindergarten teachers can also choose to earn voluntary certification through the National Board of Professional Teaching Standards (NBPTS). It is a national credential recognized by all states. The NBPTS is open to all teachers with a bachelor's degree and a minimum of three years of classroom experience in a state-approved school. Although there are 16 certification subjects, the one most relevant to teaching kindergarten is the generalist certification for early childhood. The purpose of obtaining this certification is to demonstrate expertise as a kindergarten teacher, which would increase opportunities for career advancement.

EARNINGS

THE AVERAGE SALARY FOR A KINDERGARTEN TEACHER in an American public school is about $60,000, with a range between $50,000 and $70,000. How much any individual teacher earns depends on several factors, but the most important are the number of years spent in the teaching profession and the location of the school.

Seniority Rules

Naturally, the newest kindergarten teachers earn the least. Beginner level kindergarten teachers are in the lowest 10 percentile, with starting salaries of around $40,000 on average. After a couple of years, the salary increases to nearly $45,000. Mid-level teachers, who have been on the job between five and 10 years, earn the same as the overall average of around $60,000. After 10 years of teaching, individuals are considered senior level. Their average salaries start at $70,000, and if they have credentials or specialty certifications, their annual wages may rise to as much as $90,000.

Location

Where a kindergarten teacher works can have a big impact on earnings. Salaries vary from state to state and school district to school district. Urban areas typically offer higher kindergarten teacher salaries, but then the cost of living is also higher. By contrast, a kindergarten teacher will probably earn less in a rural area where rent, food, gas, and other expenses will be lower as well.

In general, kindergarten teachers earn more in coastal states than in the South. New York pays its kindergarten teachers the most with an overall average salary of $85,000. At the other end is Mississippi where kindergarten teachers earn an average of $45,000.

In addition to New York, the highest paying states with average salaries above $70,000 are Connecticut, Massachusetts, and Oregon. California is not far behind at $65,000. The lowest paying state is Hawaii. This outlier offers its kindergarten teachers barely more than $30,000 a year on average. The next lowest is Oklahoma at $35,000. There are 17 states with average salaries under $50,000. Most of them are in the South.

Public vs Private

Kindergarten teachers at public primary schools generally fare better with their salary than those teaching at private schools. The difference is significant with kindergarten teachers at private schools averaging roughly $10,000 a year less than their public school colleagues.

Getting Through the Summer

Although public school teachers do not work during the summer, they might still get paychecks. That is because some school districts offer the option of spreading the yearly salary out over a full year so there is no gap in payments. Other districts do not give teachers a choice. They might have to accept payment over the 10 months that school is in session and figure out for themselves how to handle the two month gap. Private schools do not typically offer a way to get paychecks during the summer months off. However, these schools often need to stay open with summer programs in order to keep revenue coming in. In that case, teachers from the regular school year are offered the option to work (and earn) for part or all of the time the school is open during summer.

Benefits

Public school teachers normally receive excellent benefits packages that have been negotiated on their behalf by their unions. The two best perks are retirement plans and health insurance. The vast majority of public school teachers are enrolled in defined-benefit plans. These plans guarantee a specific payout to teachers upon retirement. The payouts are determined by a formula, which sets it apart from defined-contribution plans that pay out according to investment returns. The most common defined-contribution plan is the 401(k) account, which is ubiquitous in the private sector. Fewer than 10 percent of public school teachers participate in 401(k) plans, which are dependent on each individual teacher's personal investment decisions.

Most kindergarten teachers in public schools have exceptional healthcare coverage. However, with healthcare costs on the rise over the past 10 years, teachers have seen their contributions rising to help districts cover the costs.

Healthcare insurance for teachers in private schools ranges from having none to having full health, dental, and vision coverage. In many cases, retirement benefits are limited to voluntary participation in 401(k) plans. What and how many benefits are offered depends on where the private school is located and how much tuition students' parents are willing to pay for their child. There are many cases of part-time teachers in private schools getting virtually no benefits at all.

OPPORTUNITIES

THE JOB GROWTH RATE FOR KINDERGARTEN teachers is projected to be slow in coming decades. Any increase in demand for kindergarten teachers will come primarily from increased enrollment. As the population continues to grow, the number of students naturally grows as well. Some existing teachers will also be retiring, and their positions will need to be filled. About one third of the expected job openings will be the result of retirement. To a smaller degree, there is a growing demand for kindergarten teachers because the overall trend is to lower teacher-student ratios.

The job growth rate will vary by area of the country. Those seeking employment should consider being flexible as they may increase prospects by relocating. In general, there are far more kindergarten teachers in California, Texas, and Florida than any of the other states. The largest increase in the number of new students, however, is expected in Georgia, Texas, Nevada, and Arizona. Other Western and Southern states may also see increases in enrollment in public schools.

Teaching in public schools is in essence a government job. Therefore, employment growth often depends on state and local government budgets. Where there are budget deficits, there may be reduced job growth, a hiring freeze, or even layoffs.

For teachers wanting to work In public schools, there will be better opportunities in urban and rural school districts than in suburban school districts. Most private schools are located in affluent suburbs and upscale neighborhoods of metropolitan areas.

The demand for kindergarten teachers in private schools

is growing steadily. However, the overall number of job openings will continue to be much smaller than in the public sector. You can see the difference on any online job site. While there are literally thousands of jobs for public kindergarten teachers showing up on any job site, the same site will only show a few hundred positions in private schools.

There is plenty of competition for positions in private schools. After all, who would not prefer working with 10 or fewer well dressed, well fed kids in an immaculate classroom featuring every amenity a teacher could wish for. With these ideal circumstances, the reward is being able to easily make students (and yourself) look successful. There is a price to be paid for such a seemingly easy position. Private schools do not receive the same government support as public schools. As a result, the pay is significantly lower for kindergarten teachers in private schools.

There are always more opportunities in poorer neighborhoods where resources are limited, classes are overflowing, books are outdated, and kids depend on vouchers to get fed. It is worth considering if you want to be assured a job. In some cases, poor school districts are so desperate for teachers, they even waive the licensing requirement.

Job prospects are especially good for teachers who are bilingual, specialize in English as a Second Language (ESL), or have certification for special education.

GETTING STARTED

YOU EARNED YOUR DEGREE, COMPLETED the practice teaching, passed the exams, and now have your license to teach. It is time to land your first real teaching job. Do not expect this to be an easy task. It will take careful preparation, time, and patience, but all the hard work will be worth it. The exhilaration of landing your first kindergarten teaching job will be unforgettable.

Preparation should start while still in college with the creation of a professional teaching portfolio. A teaching portfolio provides prospective employers tangible evidence of your skills and achievements. It is a much better way to showcase your work than a simple résumé alone and is considered an essential component of the interview process. Your portfolio should include:

- Teaching goals and philosophy statements

- Copies of certifications

- A well-written résumé

- Several strong letters of recommendation

- Lesson plan examples

- Professional development activities, such as conferences, research studies, volunteer work, and mentorship

Before jumping into the job hunt, do your homework. Bone up on some teacher buzz words to show you are on top of issues in the education field. Good terms to use include discovery-based learning, balanced literacy, Bloom's taxonomy, scaffolding, multi-sensory instruction, brain break, and differentiating instruction. Make sure you know what all these mean, and sprinkle these words throughout your résumé and in interviews. Learn as much as you can about the demographic makeup of the district where you want to work. Be prepared to work that knowledge into your interview conversation and your cover letter. Make sure that you request an interview at the end of the cover letter.

Let the Job Search Begin

Check in with your college career center. You will find job openings posted, but usually only those located in close proximity to the college. However, there will also be notices of upcoming job fairs where you may find recruiters and representatives from districts you would consider.

Focus your job search online where there is a concentration of teaching jobs. Rather than the big generalized job sites, check out sites like Teacherjobs.com, educationcrossing.com, and K-12.com. There are many more job sites devoted to teachers, but these alone will bring you a massive amount of information for your job search. The search tools are very flexible. You can search by region, district, experience level, grade level, temporary or permanent positions, and more.

Another way to locate your first teaching position is to go right to the source by visiting the websites of the school districts where you would like to teach. Often, you will find links on the websites where the schools list employment opportunities in their districts.

Get in touch with your list of contacts. Reach out to people you worked for as an intern or met at professional conferences. Let them know you are ready and looking for a permanent teaching position.

Use a free recruiter. You can find one on LinkedIn. The school will pick up the tab for these services if you are hired. Some recruiters specialize in private school placements, which is particularly hard to navigate on your own.

Make yourself visible by volunteering. Look for opportunities to help out in the district where you want to teach. It could be anything – helping out in the library, a classroom, or even the lunchroom. Even a once-a-week stint will demonstrate that you really want to be there.

It may take time to find an opening in the district where you want to work. Use that time wisely by subbing. Working as a substitute teacher often does not even require a license and is a good way to get some extra experience. Plus, administrators often look to the substitute pool when hiring for a full-time position. Just make sure they know you want a permanent position; some teachers only want to be subs. Create business cards with your credentials and leave one on the desk of the teacher you subbed for and in the teachers' lounge. You will be surprised how many teachers will call you to sub for them.

ASSOCIATIONS

■ **Association of American Educators http://www.aaeteachers.org**

■ **National Association for the Education of Young Children http://www.naeyc.org**

■ **National Kindergarten Alliance https://www.nkateach.org**

WEBSITES

■ **Education Crossing**
https://www.educationcrossing.com

■ **Teacher Jobs**
https://teacherjobs.com

■ **K-12 Jobs**
https://www.k12.com/careers.html

Copyright 2020
Institute For Career Research

CAREERS INTERNET DATABASE
www.careers-internet.org